Firestone Books
Success Begins Here

An Inspector Calls
25 Key Quotations for GCSE

Mark Birch

Series Editor: Hannah Rabey

firestonebooks.com

An Inspector Calls
25 Key Quotations for GCSE
Mark Birch

Series Editor: Hannah Rabey

2020 Edition

ISBN-13: 978-1909608283

Published by Firestone Books

firestonebooks.com

You can stay up to date by following Firestone Books on Facebook and Twitter, or subscribing to our fabulous newsletter.
Go on – you know you want to…

Contents

About this Book

The GCSE English Literature exam relies on understanding a wide range of relevant references, studied both in lessons and as part of revision. This guide will provide you with in-depth analysis of 25 key quotations in J.B. Priestley's *An Inspector Calls*, written by experts to ensure that you are prepared for success.

In this guide you will find:

- A chronology of the quotations throughout the play
- A biography of J.B. Priestley's life
- A summary of the key events in each act of the play
- 25 key analysed quotations
- A key terms glossary (key terms are denoted by an asterisk)

The 25 quotations include:

- Detailed analysis of the quotation
- Key context relating to the quotation
- A list of key themes and characters that the quotation links to

A Chronology of the Quotations in this Guide

Act One

Quotation 1: 'An Inspector Calls'

Quotation 2: 'You're squiffy'

Quotation 3: '...fiddlesticks! The Germans don't want war. Nobody wants war, except some half-civilized folks in the Balkans.'

Quotation 4: '...unsinkable, absolutely unsinkable.'

Quotation 5: '...a very good chance of a knighthood – so long as we behave ourselves...'

Quotation 6: '...as if we were all mixed up together like bees in a hive – community and all that nonsense.'

Quotation 7: '...a man has to mind his own business and look after himself and his own – and – *We hear the sharp ring of a front door bell.*'

Quotation 8: 'Give us some more light.'

Quotation 9: '...it's better to ask for the earth than to take it.'

Quotation 10: '...If she'd been some miserable plain little creature, I don't suppose I'd have done it.'

Act Two

Quotation 11: 'You see, we have to share something. If there's nothing else, we'll have to share our guilt.'

Quotation 12: 'You mustn't try to build up a kind of wall between us and that girl'

Quotation 13: 'No, he's giving us the rope – so that we'll hang ourselves.'

Quotation 14: '(*staggered*) Well, really! Alderman Meggarty! I must say, we *are* learning something tonight.'

Quotation 15: 'You were the wonderful Fairy Prince. You must have adored it, Gerald.'

Quotation 16: '(massively) Public men, Mr Birling, have responsibilities as well as privileges.'

Quotation 17: 'She was claiming elaborate fine feelings and scruples that were simply absurd in a girl in her position.'

Quotation 18: '... some drunken young idler, then that's all the more reason why he shouldn't escape.'

Act Three

Quotation 19: '...you killed her – and the child she'd have had too – my child – your own grandchild you killed them both – damn you, damn you – '

Quotation 20: '...as if she were an animal, a thing, not a person'

Quotation 21: 'You made her pay a heavy price for that. And now she'll make you pay a heavier price still.'

Quotation 22: '...One Eva Smith has gone – but there are millions and millions and millions of Eva Smiths and John Smiths...with their lives, their hopes and fears, their suffering, and chance of happiness, all intertwined with our lives...'

Quotation 23: 'We don't live alone. We are members of one body. We are responsible for each other.'

Quotation 24: '...if men will not learn that lesson, then they will be taught it in fire and blood and anguish...'

Quotation 25: 'So nothing really happened. So there's nothing to be sorry for, nothing to learn. We can all go on behaving just as we did.'

A Biography of J. B. Priestley

J. B. Priestley was born in Bradford in 1894. Bradford was an important industrial town in the North of England and was an important influence on Priestley's life and work. He went to school there and began work in the wool trade after leaving education at the age of 17. Priestley witnessed first-hand the poor treatment of workers that would help to develop his social conscience.

The class system in the Edwardian era was not as rigid as it was during the reign of Queen Victoria, but society was still divided into clear groups. The wealthy and aristocratic upper classes included people like Sir George and Lady Croft. The Birlings belonged to the middle classes. The middle classes owned businesses or worked in professional occupations. The working classes still suffered significantly at this time and this ultimately led Priestley to create 'Eva Smith' in order to represent the suffering of the workers.

Priestley wished to become a writer but when the First World War began in 1914, he felt he had to sign-up. He had to face not only the horrors of war but also the class system. He felt that the 'gentlemen' who entered the army as officers were fools who sacrificed ordinary soldiers without thought or care. His sense of social injustice was reinforced by his wartime experiences. The Birlings represent the arrogance of the upper classes and their thoughtless treatment of the lower classes is one of Priestley's central themes in *An Inspector Calls*.

Priestley was wounded twice but when the war ended, he was given a grant that enabled him to study at Cambridge. He became a successful writer of critical works, novels and plays, influenced by famous socialist* writers of the time such as George Bernard Shaw and H.G. Wells, who also became personal friends. When the character of Arthur Birling states 'We can't let these Bernard Shaws and H. G. Wellses do all the talking,' Priestley is contrasting the political position of the self-proclaimed 'hard-headed, practical man of business' and the notable socialist thinkers whose views were very similar to Priestley's own.

Priestley married in 1921. Despite discovering that his wife was suffering from terminal cancer in 1924, he engaged in a number of affairs, an experience that may have influenced his representation of infidelity in the character of Gerald in *An Inspector Calls*.

Priestley wrote a number of plays that dealt with the theme of time and the responsibility for an individual's actions over time. The most famous of these, *Time and the Conways* and *I Have Been Here Before,* were both written in 1937. He was heavily influenced by the writings of J.W. Dunne, who explored an idea of time in which the past, present and future are blurred. He believed that dreams provide a chance to see into our own futures. The work of P.D. Ouspensky also had an impact on Priestley. Ouspensky believed that life was relived many times and that intelligent people could sometimes perceive moments from their other lives. He claimed that 'chosen' people recognised this process and could intervene in other people's lives to prevent terrible mistakes from being made. It could be argued that Priestley presents the Inspector as one of these 'chosen' people and, in common with Dunne's beliefs, the narrative's use of time, with its cyclical pattern, blurs the boundary between past, present and future. The play's structure provides an opportunity for events to recur, providing another opportunity for the Birlings to learn from their mistakes.

During the Second World War, Priestley presented the BBC radio programme *Postscripts*. The audience was enormous, with Priestley's audience share being second only to that of Prime Minister Winston Churchill's official statements to the nation. In the programmes, Priestley explored the effects of the war in a way that increased the morale of the British people but he also increasingly expressed his socialist ideology; one could argue that Priestley's community-minded principles that he presented in his popular

Postscripts contributed to the Labour Party's landslide victory in the 1945 general election. This would have represented a victory for Priestley's socialist beliefs that he would then attempt to justify in the production of *An Inspector Calls*.

An Inspector Calls was written within a single week, but no London theatre was available to stage it. Priestley later stated that 'the Red Army being much in our minds at that time, I sent a copy to Moscow.' It was immediately translated and staged in Moscow in 1945 by two companies at the same time, before being performed by the Old Vic Company in London in 1946.

Priestley continued to write a great deal after the Second World War, receiving many forms of acclaim. In 1977 the Queen made him a member of the Order of Merit. He died in 1984.

A Summary of the Key Events in *An Inspector Calls*

Act One

- The Birling family celebrate the engagement of their daughter, Sheila, to Gerald Croft.
- Mr Arthur Birling makes a speech about the state of the country.
- After Shelia accepts Gerald's ring, the women leave and Mr Birling informs Gerald of the possibility that he might be awarded a knighthood.
- The Inspector arrives, showing Mr Birling a photograph of a girl who has died.
- The Inspector explains Mr Birling's part in her death, given that he sacked her from his factory after she fought for a wage rise.
- Sheila returns and is shown a photograph that is hidden from the other characters.
- The Inspector explains Sheila's involvement in the girl's life: she insisted on the girl being sacked from Milwards' department store.
- The Inspector shocks Gerald when he explains that the girl changed her name to Daisy Renton.

Act Two

- Gerald explains how he met 'Daisy' in the Palace bar and began a relationship with her.
- Sheila returns Gerald's ring and Gerald leaves.
- Mrs Sybil Birling admits that she persuaded the Brumley Women's Charity Organisation to deny Eva Smith's request for help.

- The Inspector reveals that Eva was pregnant.
- Mrs Birling blames the father of the child, stating that Eva's suicide was his responsibility.
- Mrs Birling is shocked to realise that the father is Eric.

Act Three

- Eric returns and recognises that the others already understand his guilt.
- Eric explains how he met Eva Smith at the Palace bar and forced his way into her lodgings where he had sex with her.
- Eric reveals that Eva Smith was pregnant and that he took money from his father's business to support her.
- Eva Smith refused the money offered by Eric and sought help from the Brumley Women's Charity Organisation.
- Eric blames his mother for Eva's death.
- After concluding that we are all responsible for each other, the Inspector leaves.
- Gerald returns, having spoken to a police sergeant, and confirms Sheila's suspicion that Inspector Goole was not a real inspector.
- Gerald questions whether they have been referring to the same girl.
- Gerald rings the infirmary and confirms that no-one has committed suicide.
- Mr Birling, Mrs Birling and Gerald celebrate. The Birlings receive a phone call that reveals that a girl has died on the way to the infirmary and a police inspector is on his way to ask them questions.

An Inspector Calls

25 Key Quotations for GCSE

Quotation 1

Act 1

Title:

"An Inspector Calls"

Analysis

The title of the play is one of the most significant quotations. It centres the play's position within the detective genre, a genre that was very popular during the 1940s when the play was written and first performed. This genre has clear conventions*, including the arrival of a detective who interviews suspects in order to solve a crime (usually a murder) and often featuring a concluding narrative twist. Priestley manipulates audience expectations by both conforming to the conventions of the detective genre and undermining them, making the narrative twists even more unexpected and shocking. In a sense, the play is not what it appears to be, in the same way that the characters are not what they appear to be.

A sense of mystery is created through the vague nature of the title. There is no sense of what has happened, and the entire focus is on the character of the Inspector. The word 'Inspector' is ambiguous* as it denotes both a police rank and also one who inspects, a point that Sheila refers to in response to her father's rejection of Goole's Inspector status, when she states: 'Well, he inspected us all right.' The title emphasises the significance of the Inspector's arrival given that, structurally, from the point at which 'An Inspector Calls', the lives of each of the characters in the play changes. *An Inspector Calls* is often regarded as a 'well-made play*'. Part of this categorisation involves a move from ignorance to knowledge (anagnorisis*) for both the characters and audience. This process begins when the Inspector calls and it is the Inspector who is used by Priestley to transfer knowledge.

Priestley's use of the indefinite article* 'An' is significant as Priestley sought to gain support for socialist beliefs, so the indefinite article universalises this, suggesting that the message is more important rather than the identity of any one Inspector. This is complemented by the use of the present-tense verb 'Calls', representing the message as one of timeless importance. The use of the present tense could also foreshadow the significance of time in the play. Priestley's interest in the theories of Dunne and Ouspensky, represented in the cyclical* nature of the narrative, could be symbolically conveyed by the simple present verb's association with action that happens again and again. Time is also significant in that the play conforms to the 'Unities*' of Classical tragedy derived from Aristotle's *Poetics*: time, place and action. The play takes place within the space of a single evening, in real time; it centres on one place (the Birlings' dining room); and the action is continuous.

The verb 'Calls' is ambiguous. An obvious meaning is its denotation* of a brief social 'call', but this is highly euphemistic and potentially ironic, given the Inspector's brutally honest judgement of the Birlings. Once again, the expectations of the audience are set up in order to be undermined. 'Calls' could also refer to a demand for attention or action, reflecting the moral demands made by the Inspector before his departure.

Key Characters	Key Themes
Inspector Goole	Judgement Responsibility

Quotation 2 | Act 1

Sheila Birling:

"You're Squiffy"

Analysis

The word 'squiffy' is a colloquial* slang word of the Edwardian* period, meaning 'slightly intoxicated' and derived from 'skew-whiff'. The word's use is criticised by Mrs Birling, despite it being a mild euphemism, as something inappropriate for a girl of Sheila's class to use. This criticism of language is typical of Mrs Birling's obsession with the surface appearance of respectability. Her criticism of her daughter's language also highlights her lack of genuine compassion; she convinces herself that Eric is not an alcoholic and does not criticise her son's drinking perhaps because this would mean accepting the reality of the situation: that her son's behaviour is not appropriate for someone of his class. In contrast, criticising Sheila's use of mild language helps Mrs Birling to reinforce the social expectations that she believes define her class.

The exchange between Sheila and Eric suggests the nature of the sibling relationship. They appear competitive, with the short declarative sentences giving a sense of the certainty of Sheila's statement echoed by Eric's 'I'm not.'

The statement 'You're squiffy' is the first clear indication of Eric's excessive drinking for the audience but the use of euphemism to convey it suggests that the drinking is tolerated or overlooked. In Act Two, Sheila clarifies that 'He's been steadily drinking too much for the last two years.' The emotional distance between members of the family is evident in Mrs Birling's apparent lack of knowledge of this drinking and Sheila's long period of ignoring it. The Edwardian period was characterised by this kind of repression of distasteful subjects. The euphemistic language is also used by Eric in his admission of guilt regarding his treatment of Eva Smith: 'I was a bit squiffy', mitigating the significance of his actions. Other euphemisms are used by characters to disguise the prejudices of the upper classes, such as: 'It's a favourite haunt of women of the town', 'a girl of that class' and Mrs Birling's description of Eva's pregnancy as 'that particular condition.'

Key Characters

Eric Birling
Sheila Birling
Sybil Birling

Key Themes

Age
Judgement
Social Class

Quotation 3 | Act 1

Arthur Birling:

"...fiddlesticks! The Germans don't want war. Nobody wants war, except some half-civilized folks in the Balkans."

Analysis

This quotation forms part of a very long speech by Arthur Birling that illustrates his arrogance. He speaks at length about politics, an inappropriate subject for his daughter's engagement party. His selfishness is clear through his focus on his own interests rather than the celebration of Gerald's proposal. The sheer length of the speech displays a pompous self-interest. While the comments made by other characters never exceed five words during the speech, Mr Birling's speech extends to over 500 words. Birling even begins by telling Sheila that he will make the speech 'at' her, rather than 'for' her.

Mr Birling's interjection*, 'fiddlesticks!', reveals the extent of his arrogance. He is so dismissive of the idea that the Germans might want war that he feels it is appropriate to use a term that mocks the very idea. The epistrophe* of 'want war...wants war' serves to stress the significance of war through the word's repetition, also complementing Birling's claim that a rejection of war is universal. This is a very clear example of dramatic irony since the first performance of the play was the year after the end of the Second

World War. The audience would recognise that Birling is wrong and Priestley's presentation of Birling's arrogant certainty mocks both the character and those in society that he represents. Priestley effectively makes the audience laugh at the character of Mr Birling and his views, helping them to appreciate that Birling should be regarded as naïve for the rest of the play.

Many people at the time the play is set displayed ignorance of what was happening internationally and its potential impact on Britain. Mocking Birling's arrogant judgements, from the exposition of the play, allows Priestley to highlight his moral message: concerns about war and the rise of the right-wing* should never be ignored. Undermining the significance of what is happening internationally can lead to horrors such as the First World War.

Birling's own ignorance extends to racism in the phrase 'half-civilized folks in the Balkans.' His beliefs are grounded in old-fashioned prejudices about the superiority of the British. He is likely to be referring to the First Balkan War, which took place between 1912 and 1913, at around the date that the play is set. The Balkan League consisted of the forces of Bulgaria, Greece, Montenegro and Serbia, so Birling is potentially condemning a wide range of people as 'half-civilized'.

Key Characters
Arthur Birling

Key Themes
Judgement

Quotation 4 | Act 1

Arthur Birling:

"...unsinkable, absolutely unsinkable."

Analysis

The reference to the Titanic 'sailing next week' allows Priestley to set the play at a specific, identifiable time, making it more realistic. This realism makes the play's moral message profound and its narrative twist more shocking.

The 'unsinkable' Titanic sank on its maiden voyage in 1912, just a week after the setting of the play, killing over 1,500 people. The ship was regarded as an important symbol of capitalist* accomplishment, technological advancement and luxury. The ship fostered great pride, as evidenced by Arthur Birling, who functions as Priestley's personification of capitalism. The sinking of the 'indestructible' ship shocked the world, causing widespread outrage over the lack of lifeboats, lax regulations and the unequal treatment of the three passenger classes during the evacuation. The sinking of RMS Titanic revealed the hubris of the industrialists who had constructed it. It was this hubris that many regarded as the cause for so much unnecessary loss of life. The anger felt towards these industrialists would have been applied to Birling, particularly by the play's early audiences, as he exhibited the same hubris and misplaced optimism.

Birling's misplaced optimism is also symbolically doomed to sink under the interrogation of the Inspector. It is the failure to question and the foolish arrogance seen in such examples of capitalism, that Priestley wishes to expose.

This is one of the clearest examples of dramatic irony in the play. Once again, the audience is invited to mock the attitudes expressed by Birling and what his character represents: capitalism.

Priestley's use of epistrophe, coupled with the intensifying adverb 'absolutely', reinforces Birling's certainty and, in the light of the dramatic irony, his misplaced arrogance.

It may be significant that, proportionally, many more first-class passengers on the Titanic survived. Priestley's construction of Eva Smith, a working-class woman, to highlight the conditions of many in British society, mirrors the way in which the most vulnerable in Edwardian society suffered the most in the tragedy of the Titanic.

Key Characters

Arthur Birling

Eva Smith

Key Themes

Responsibility

Social Class

Quotation 5 | Act 1

Arthur Birling:

"...a very good chance of a knighthood – so long as we behave ourselves..."

Analysis

Mr Birling is presented as a weak character. For all his boasting and arrogance, he recognises that he is the social inferior of the Crofts. He is desperate to impress them through the possibility of receiving a knighthood in the next Honours List. As soon as he has the opportunity to speak to Gerald alone, he informs him of this possibility and despite stating that the information should remain confidential, he quickly accepts the idea that Gerald should 'drop a hint' to his mother. Mr Birling is concerned with appearance rather than reality.

Birling's arrogance is evident, once again, as he is prepared to foster the idea of receiving this honour when, by his own admission, it is only a 'chance'. He also insincerely dismisses the value of the honour through the reference to it as 'just' a knighthood. The way that Mr Birling has proudly taken the opportunity to tell Gerald about the knighthood undermines his false modesty.

Priestley may have chosen this particular honour as it is associated with the role of medieval knights. It was a duty of knights to defend and support women. It is deeply ironic that Birling should regard himself as fitting to receive this honour, given his treatment of Eva Smith and other women like her.

The dramatic irony is clearly revealed through Birling's qualifying statement: 'so long as we behave ourselves.' Given that the audience know, from the title of the play, that an Inspector is about to arrive, it should come as no surprise that the Birlings have not behaved themselves. This follows other examples of dramatic irony in the exposition of the play that reveal Birling's lack of judgement. Priestley may be guiding the audience to an understanding that Birling's belief that he is due a knighthood is just one more error of judgement.

Key Characters

Arthur Birling

Key Themes

Judgement

Social Class

Quotation 6 | Act 1

Arthur Birling:

"...as if we were all mixed up together like bees in a hive – community and all that nonsense."

Analysis

By the time *An Inspector Calls* was written, Britain had already suffered a terrible economic depression. The effects of this were worsened by the lack of any real welfare state. Homelessness and crime had increased, causing issues for the working classes in particular. The capitalist system that Mr Birling symbolically represents was blamed for the depression by many at the time.

Birling's words are presented as a criticism of socialist beliefs. Expressed in a mocking tone, his words reject the idea of community by dismissively associating it with 'all that nonsense.' This is another example of Birling's arrogance. He believes himself to be superior to other members of society and that, as a result, he should not be forced to mix with them.

The zoomorphic* simile 'like bees in a hive' presents Mr Birling's attempt to belittle the socialist principle of equality by reducing its idea of community to the behaviour of insects. However, Birling's imagery undermines this concept as bees work together highly effectively, with very positive outcomes. 'Mixed up' also connotes disorder, something that is at odds with the image of productivity conveyed by the bees simile. He also ironically uses the collective pronoun 'we'. The pronoun is plural so refers to a number of people, but it is used by Mr Birling when he is rejecting collectivism. Priestley may be mocking Arthur Birling himself by presenting him as mocking an idea through imagery and language that does not serve his purpose.

Key Characters
Arthur Birling

Key Themes
Responsibility
Social Class

Quotation 7 | Act 1

Arthur Birling:

"...a man has to mind his own business and look after himself and his own – and –

We hear the sharp ring of a front door bell."

Analysis

Mr Birling's didactic* speech to Eric and Gerald ends with this statement that summarises his philosophy of individualism and personal responsibility. He claims to have learnt this through experience, elevating his views above those of the 'youngsters' whose views are implied to be naïve. The arrogance of Birling is represented through the polysyndetic* list used. He appears to be in the middle of a seemingly endless list of his own social rules when he is interrupted by the doorbell. Even before this interruption, Priestley uses staged pauses, in the form of dashes, to indicate that Birling is struggling to find the words that his egotism demands for a lengthy speech.

The diegetic sound* of the bell symbolises the arrival of the Inspector. Even before entering the house, the Inspector has interrupted Birling, ending his monologue. Given that the Inspector is a vehicle for the socialist views of Priestley, the nature of his arrival could convey the way in which his socialism* will cut off the capitalism that Arthur Birling represents. Priestley is representing the powerful authority of the Inspector even before his entrance.

In Act Three, Sheila uses the 'queer' timing of this entrance as justification for her view that the Inspector might not have been a real inspector.

The use of the adjective 'sharp' to describe the bell, conveys the painful lesson to be delivered by the Inspector. It will soon be complemented by the change to 'brighter and harder' lighting to signal the Inspector's arrival, and the imminent exposure of the family's wrongdoings. The sharpness of the 'ring' also serves to aurally impact on the audience. It alerts the audience to the significance of the Inspector's entrance.

When Eric quotes his father, shortly after the Inspector's arrival, stating: '...as you were saying, Dad, a man has to look after himself –', Mr Birling is presented as embarrassed by his own words, dismissing them with 'we needn't go into all that.' His capitalist views already appear to have been shaken. In Act Three, Eric confronts his father about this, saying 'I didn't notice you told him that it's every man for himself.' The Inspector has undermined the authority of Mr Birling with the younger members of the family.

Key Characters

Arthur Birling
Eric Birling
Inspector Goole

Key Themes

Age
Responsibility

Quotation 8	Act 1

Arthur Birling:

"Give us some more light."

Analysis

The opening stage directions refer to the lighting being 'pink and intimate' until the Inspector's arrival. It is at this point that it becomes 'brighter and harder'. The lighting symbolises the tone of the play, with the artificial optimism and harmony of the Birlings conveyed through the warm, intimate lighting and the brightness of the light upon the Inspector's arrival representing the manner in which truth is exposed, or literally 'brought to light'.

It is ironic that this literal light should be demanded by Mr Birling when the Inspector will turn the metaphorical light of exposure upon Mr Birling first of all. The National Theatre production heightens this sense of exposure for the audience by using this command to literally open up the Birlings' house to the audience.

Mr Birling directs his imperative* 'Give' to Edna, with no politeness codes being used. This may demonstrate Mr Birling's sense of superiority over the working classes and his lack of consideration for them. Given the phonological similarity* between 'Edna' and 'Eva', the two working-class female characters in the play,

Priestley may intend the audience to recognise that Mr Birling's treatment of the working classes is universalised. His approach to the working classes, in general, is authoritarian and inhumane. Priestley may be using this as a way of criticising Edwardian and post-war attitudes to class. A visual contrast to this inhumane approach is provided in the National Theatre production, when the Inspector offers a deprived street-child an apple and affectionately ruffles his hair. The Inspector and Mr Birling are represented as opposing forces with their opposition based on political views. Mr Birling represents capitalism and the Inspector represents socialism.

Key Characters

Arthur Birling
Eva Smith
Inspector Goole

Key Themes

Judgement
Social Class

Quotation 9	Act 1

Inspector Goole:

"...it's better to ask for the earth than to take it."

Analysis

The Inspector's words are a response to Mr Birling's claim that 'If you don't come down sharply on some of these people, they'd soon be asking for the earth.' Mr Birling's emphasis is on the metaphor of the earth as a symbol of something vast. He believes that it is necessary to 'come down sharply' on his workers in order to stop them wanting more, using the hyperbolic* metaphor of 'the earth' to suggest that their demands will be totally unreasonable.

The Inspector deconstructs Birling's use of this idiom*, placing his focus on the verb 'asking'. Priestley uses the vehicle of the Inspector to note that the workers have asked for greater fairness rather than having taken their share of the nation's wealth by force. Priestley may be drawing upon his interest in Russia, as the Russian Revolution of 1917 was still a recent memory for a post-war audience. While this event took place after the period in which the play is set, Priestley's contemporary audience would have been very aware of the events in which the workers overthrew Russia's monarchy and capitalist class. The parallels between the position of Mr Birling as the capitalist businessman restricting the flow of wealth to the workers would be apparent to many, as would the link between the strike-leader Eva Smith and the striking Russian workers who were at the heart of the Revolution. Priestley could be offering a warning that if society does not change then revolution could spread to Britain.

A secondary interpretation is that the Inspector is referring to Arthur Birling himself as one who has taken 'the earth'. He is the one with great wealth, who has benefitted from the capitalist system while denying the workers' fair pay.

The comparative adjective and the parallelism* within this speech force the audience to consider the contrast between the sense of respect that is clear in 'ask' and the selfishness of 'take' (whether this is the workers being forced to take a fair share or a criticism of the upper classes having already taken more than their fair share).

Key Characters

Inspector Goole

Arthur Birling

Key Themes

Social Class

Quotation 10 | Act 1

Sheila Birling:

"If she'd been some miserable plain little creature, I don't suppose I'd have done it."

Analysis

An Inspector Calls displays the conventions of a variety of different dramatic forms, one of which is the morality play. Morality plays aimed to teach the audience lessons based on the seven deadly sins: gluttony, greed, lust, sloth, wrath, envy and pride. Characters who displayed these sins would receive punishment unless they asked for forgiveness. Each of the characters inspected in the play exhibit at least one of the seven deadly sins, with Sheila being guilty of envy and wrath (anger) when dealing with Eva Smith.

Sheila's envy is apparent when she admits that her behaviour would have been different if Eva was a 'plain little creature'. Her focus on appearance is clear from the use of 'plain' but her wrath is also still in evidence, despite the incident having taken place well over a year before, through the use of the diminutive* 'little' to modify the zoomorphic 'creature'. All three words reveal her disrespect. She still feels the anger that comes from the unflattering comparison between herself and Eva.

In the heavily patriarchal* Edwardian era, a woman's value would be determined to some extent by her looks. In a capitalist and patriarchal economy, a woman could secure her economic prospects through marriage. Sheila's envy of Eva, despite Eva's far lower social status, may be regarded as a result of this kind of society. The fact that Gerald has an affair with Eva provides Priestley with an opportunity to criticise treatment of women, from what we may now class as a feminist perspective. Eva's ability to secure her future on the basis of her looks seems to be what Sheila refers to when she claims that Eva 'looked as if she could take care of herself.' Eva is able to gain the interest of someone from the upper classes, like Gerald, due to her looks. However, she is disposed of when she becomes an inconvenience.

Shelia's self-awareness and acceptance of what she has done wrong provide a route for her redemption that is shared by Eric. Priestley seems to be suggesting that within the context of a morality play, the younger generation provide hope for the future.

The didactic function of the morality play would have appealed to Priestley's desire for social reform and justice. Judgements made about the Birlings by the audience might also be applied to the audience members themselves, forcing them to question their own behaviour and provide the opportunity for them to question their own moral choices.

Key Characters

Eva Smith

Sheila Birling

Key Themes

Age

Social Class

Responsibility

Quotation 11 | Act 2

Inspector Goole:

"You see, we have to share something. If there's nothing else, we'll have to share our guilt."

Analysis

After Sheila accepts her responsibility, the Inspector defends her right to remain in the room so that she does not feel that the responsibility for Eva's death is hers alone. He addresses Sheila and Gerald 'sternly', emphasising the seriousness of his moral point. His comments do not seem appropriate to the traditional role of an Inspector given that they concern morality rather than culpability. Sheila's suspicions regarding the Inspector's identity are clearly fuelled by his comments as she follows them by 'wonderingly' stating 'I don't understand about you.'

Inspector Goole's statement is a subtle declaration of the need for socialism. The plural pronoun 'we' and the verb 'share', both convey the sense of community that lies at the heart of socialism. They are repeated in a form of parallelism that complements the sense of order, equality and harmony that a socialist ideal represents.

A principle of socialism is that wealth should be shared. However, the Inspector points out that when this does not occur, there is 'Nothing else' to share aside from guilt. In an Edwardian society that does not protect its weaker members and where the distribution of wealth is unfair, the message conveyed by the Inspector is that all are responsible and bear the guilt of the suffering that follows.

The conditional clause* 'If there's nothing else' could offer hope for the future. *An Inspector Calls* was written just before the landslide Labour party victory in the 1945 general election so the possibility of the country moving towards a fairer society, governed by an ideology of collective responsibility, may have provided the hope for there actually being another possibility for the future of the country.

The Inspector's certainty that collectivism is necessary is clear in his use of the auxiliary verb 'have'. The Inspector, as Priestley's mouthpiece, stresses the necessity of having to 'share', whether this is the sharing of the means of production or the sharing of emotions such as love and compassion. The fate of Eva Smith is a result of each character's failures but, without change, the Birlings and the audience will share the guilt for the continuation of an unfair society.

Key Characters
Inspector Goole

Key Themes
Responsibility

Quotation 12 | Act 2

Sheila Birling:

"You mustn't try to build up a kind of wall between us and that girl."

Analysis

Sheila's statement follows her interruption of her mother's dismissive comments ('girls of that class') regarding the death of Eva Smith. While Sheila's use of the determiner 'that' echoes her mother's use of the same word, Mrs Birling was in the process of making an offensive remark about a whole class of people, separating herself from them. In contrast, Sheila's comment is an appeal for inclusivity and the breaking down of barriers. Here, Priestley presents hope for society in the form of a younger generation who are prepared to break away from the narrow-minded generalisations of the older generation.

The metaphor of the wall may represent the more clearly constructed class boundaries that existed in Edwardian society. Presenting this boundary as a 'wall' conveys its solidity and inflexible nature. This is a difficult barrier to overcome. Sheila attempts to stop her mother from reinforcing these divisions, extending the metaphor through the image of her mother trying to 'build up' the wall.

Sheila's moral certainty is represented through the use of the modal verb 'must'. She has already been persuaded by the Inspector's methods. This fuels her increasing determination to challenge her mother's stubbornness.

Sheila returns to this metaphor shortly afterwards, within the context of denying Eric's alcoholism. She refers to building up a wall that's 'sure to be knocked flat. It makes it all the harder to bear.' Walls are false divisions and Sheila appears to have recognised that hiding from the truth is doomed to failure. Attempts to hide from reality only make the inevitable revelation of the truth more painful.

Key Characters

Sheila Birling

Sybil Birling

Key Themes

Age

Social Class

Quotation 13 | Act 2

Sheila Birling:

"No, he's giving us the rope – so that we'll hang ourselves."

Analysis

Mr Birling introduces the metaphor of 'rope' in order to suggest to the Inspector that he does not intend to give him much more freedom to pursue his enquiries. To 'give' rope in this context suggests a loosening that metaphorically conveys freedom. The Inspector's response that 'You needn't give me any rope,' reinforces Priestley's representation of the power of the Inspector. He does not need Birling's authority. There is a sense that he has already made a judgement regarding the Birlings.

Sheila's response transforms the metaphor of giving rope as a symbol of freedom into an allusion to the well-known idiom 'Give him enough rope and he'll hang himself'. The connotations* are directly opposed, as are the older and younger generations' attitudes. Sheila's character is depicted as perceptive. She fully appreciates that the Birlings are condemning themselves through their comments to the Inspector. In contrast, Mr Birling is ignorant, believing himself to have the power to control the Inspector.

It is ironic that the idiom used by Sheila to reveal her understanding of the Inspector is one that is based on an image of suicide. The Inspector is, on the surface, investigating a suicide and Sheila's comment draws a parallel between the fate of the girl and the fate of the Birlings, although Eva Smith is condemned by society and the Birlings are condemned by their own selfishness.

Key Characters

Arthur Birling
Inspector Goole
Sheila Birling

Key Themes

Age
Judgement

Quotation 14 | Act 2

Sybil Birling:

"(*staggered*) Well, really! Alderman Meggarty! I must say, we *are* learning something tonight."

Analysis

Mrs Birling is shocked that Gerald describes Joe Meggarty as a 'notorious womaniser as well as being one of the worst sots and rogues in Brumley.' Priestley's stage direction, 'staggered' reveals that this is one of the greatest shocks experienced by Mrs Birling. In fact, it is the same stage direction used by Priestley to reveal Mrs Birling's shock at the revelation that Eric is an alcoholic. However, here she is surprised because this kind of behaviour is attributed to someone of the upper classes. Mrs Birling is classist. She has to clarify that Gerald is referring to 'Alderman' Meggarty as his social position (an alderman being a high-status member of the council) makes him a member of her own class. She considers herself, and people like her, to be superior to the working classes. Priestley portrays Mrs Birling to be a bigot throughout the play. Eva Smith is dismissed by her as '...a girl of that sort...' Eva Smith's class, in Mrs Birling's eyes, condemns her to moral as well as financial inferiority. Mrs Birling's shock is also conveyed by her use of minor, exclamatory sentences*. It is as if the shock is so great, that she cannot express herself. The central irony within Priestley's drama is that it is precisely these 'superior' characters who demonstrate the most appalling behaviours.

The Edwardian era expected high standards of morality from its public figures yet here Priestley reveals that the immorality of such figures extends well beyond the Birlings. Mrs Birling is aristocratic and the Chair of the Brumley Women's Charity Organisation. Her husband was Lord Mayor and is still a magistrate. Also, the behaviour of both Eric Birling and Gerald Croft have similarities with the behaviour of Alderman Meggarty. All three go to the Palace bar, a place notorious for prostitution, and are guilty of abusing their positions with their exploitative sexual behaviour. By representing the immorality of a wide range of characters from the upper classes of Brumley society, Priestley presents a powerful form of social criticism.

It is also deeply ironic that Mrs Birling says 'we *are* learning something' when that is precisely what she is not doing. The stress on the auxiliary verb may suggest an ironic tone yet Priestley invites the audience, through this, to ironically mock Mrs Birling's prejudices*. She is given information but refuses to learn from it, as Priestley reveals in Act Three.

Key Characters

Eric Birling
Gerald Croft
Sybil Birling

Key Themes

Judgement
Social Class

Quotation 15 | Act 2

Sheila Birling:

"You were the wonderful Fairy Prince. You must have adored it, Gerald."

Analysis

Priestley describes Sheila saying this with 'sharp sarcasm'. The adjective 'sharp' may be used to represent both the pain that Sheila feels at Gerald's betrayal and the pain that she wishes Gerald to feel because of his actions. The sarcasm is reinforced through the adjective 'wonderful' and the verb 'adored' given that they both convey powerful positive feelings that Gerald does not deserve. Sheila believes that Gerald is vain, so he would have adored Eva Smith's attention. Ironically, vanity is the main sin that Sheila is guilty of in her treatment of Eva Smith.

The metaphor of Gerald as the 'Fairy Prince' conveys Sheila's belief that he would be seen, by a working-class girl, as a fantasy figure: wealthy and aristocratic. He could have inspired adoration because his wealth and power would have made him seem to be other-worldly. He has also fulfilled the role of a 'handsome prince' in a fairy-tale in seemingly rescuing Daisy/Eva, a damsel in distress, from Alderman Meggarty. This is a role that Gerald has exploited. He admits that he did not feel for Daisy/Eva what she felt for him and he abandons her when the owner of the flat he has loaned to Daisy/Eva is due to return.

The representation of Gerald's infidelity is likely to have been shaped by Priestley's own infidelities. Priestley demonstrates an awareness of the harm caused by being unfaithful, but he also permits Gerald the opportunity for forgiveness, from both Sheila and the Inspector, on the basis of his apparent honesty and that he 'had some affection for her.'

Key Characters

Gerald Croft

Sheila Birling

Key Themes

Judgement

Quotation 16 | Act 2

Inspector Goole:

"(*massively*) Public men, Mr Birling, have responsibilities as well as privileges."

Analysis

Priestley introduces the Inspector to the play by describing him as creating 'an impression of massiveness'. Afterwards, Priestley refers to the Inspector's actions through the adverb 'massively' several times. The frequency of this word's use illustrates its importance to Priestley. The Inspector should dominate the narrative, controlling the action of the play. The fact that the adverb usually modifies a verb, that also suggests dominance, complements this effect. The Inspector is described as 'cutting through massively', 'cutting in massively' and 'massively taking charge' before he makes this statement. The declarative is presented as a fact, both in terms of its content and its delivery. It is interesting that the Inspector's comment seems self-evident yet Mr Birling's response of 'Possibly' is shockingly uncertain. Mr Birling seems reluctant to accept the responsibility that his position in society requires.

The Inspector's domination of the situation defuses the anger of both Mr and Mrs Birling at this point in the play. 'Public men' is a reference to those who hold a public office, such as mayor or magistrate. The Inspector undermines the implicit claim of Mr

Birling that he should be respected because of his public office, asserting his power by interrupting Mr Birling's speech and rejecting this demand for respect by stating that those who hold positions of power should be responsible for the use of that power. The Inspector has essentially stated that Mr Birling is not only responsible for what he did to Eva Smith, but that he has a wider responsibility for those like her as a result of his position. He has failed, in both respects, to honour the demands of his position.

This notion of the responsibilities of 'public men' would have been recognised as a cultural legacy of Victorian values. The belief was that the upper classes should take responsibility for the welfare of the lower classes. The audience would be very aware that Mr Birling enjoys the privileges that are associated with his position. The play's opening stage directions draw attention to the prosperity that Mr Birling enjoys from his business. Birling has accepted all of the privileges of his position but rejected the responsibilities. Priestley uses this as a form of social criticism.

Key Characters
Arthur Birling
Inspector Goole

Key Themes
Responsibility

Quotation 17	Act 2

Sybil Birling:

"She was claiming elaborate fine feelings and scruples that were simply absurd in a girl in her position."

Analysis

Priestley presents Mrs Birling as an unsympathetic character. She is selfish, arrogant and displays class prejudice. Before condemning Eva Smith, she defends herself by blaming her own husband for Eva's situation. This ability to turn on her own family and to blame anyone except herself is deeply ironic given her claim that 'scruples' would be absurd for Eva 'in her position'. 'Scruples' refers to feelings that stop someone from doing something that they believe to be wrong. Mrs Birling clearly believes she has these 'scruples' but also believes that the lower classes do not have such morals. Ironically, it is Eva Smith who we later learn who had strong morals, doing what is right, by refusing Eric's stolen money.

Priestley makes the audience aware of Mrs Birling's insistence on social respectability and 'fine feelings' early in Act One when she criticises her husband for suggesting complimenting his own cook. She also appears appalled at Sheila's use of the word 'squiffy'. These 'fine feelings' are superficial and based on social politeness codes* but Priestley represents the way in which true moral character is revealed under pressure, either from the Inspector or circumstances. Eva Smith demonstrates the honesty of the working classes whilst Mrs Birling represents the ruthlessness of the upper classes.

The phrase 'in her position' is ambiguous. Mrs Birling could be referring to Eva's poverty, class or pregnancy. She believes that it is ridiculous that anyone who is in such a difficult position could have any values. This belief conveys her own prejudices. Priestley's ironic representation of Mrs Birling can be seen in her behaviour as Chair of the Brumley Women's Charity Organisation. She is completely lacking in charity. It seems that she uses her role not to help others but to use power, denying support to someone in need because of her own class prejudice.

Eva Smith's moral behaviour is something that Mrs Birling would regard as suited to someone of the upper classes and she therefore states that Eva is lying. She cannot believe that 'a girl in her position' would turn down money. Her complete disbelief is emphasised by changing 'absurd' to the adverb 'simply'. Eva's true crime, in the eyes of Mrs Birling, is having ideas above her station, believing herself to have the integrity that Mrs Birling only assigns to the upper classes. The implication that they are in some way equal appals Mrs Birling. It is the same horror of potential equality that she felt in hearing Eva name herself 'Mrs Birling' and the same horror felt by some of the upper classes when the Inspector questions the social hierarchy through his claim that 'We are members of one body.'

Key Characters

Eva Smith
Sybil Birling

Key Themes

Judgement
Responsibility
Social Class

Quotation 18	Act 2

Sybil Birling:

"...some drunken young idler, then that's all the more reason why he shouldn't escape."

Analysis

Priestley has already prepared the audience to identify Eric as a 'drunken young idler' through his 'squiffy' behaviour in Act One and Sheila's identification of him as 'steadily drinking too much for the last two years'. Priestley uses dramatic irony* through Mrs Birling failing to recognise Eric as the 'drunken young idler' she refers to. Mrs Birling has access to much of the same information as the audience, but she refuses to accept or even to see the truth that the audience sees so readily. This is typical of Mrs Birling's character. She is blind to her son's drinking; blind to the immorality of the upper classes symbolised by the behaviour of Alderman Meggarty and the Birlings' 'respectable friends'; blind to the class prejudice that she is subject to; and blind to her own responsibilities.

Her failure to recognise the description of her own son also confirms the detachment between mother and son. The lack of openness in this relationship can also be seen between Sheila and Mrs Birling when Sheila tells Eric 'I could have told her months ago, but of course I didn't.' The alienation of the younger generation from their parents is also paralleled in Eric's statement to his father that '...you're not the kind of father a chap could go to.'

Mrs Birling unknowingly condemns her son by identifying him as a 'drunken idler'. The alienation of the younger generation is made explicit by Mrs Birling singling out 'young' as an adjective to reinforce the sins of gluttony and sloth referred to in 'drunken' and 'idler'. She judges the young as being sinful.

Mr Birling appears to confirm his wife's unwitting judgement of Eric by stating that Eric had been 'spoilt'. This criticism ironically places the blame for Eric's behaviour on his parents.

Key Characters

Arthur Birling
Eric Birling
Sybil Birling

Key Themes

Age
Judgement
Responsibility
Social Class

Quotation 19	Act 3

Eric Birling:

"...you killed her – and the child she'd have had too – my child – your own grandchild – you killed them both – damn you, damn you –"

Analysis

The frequent dashes that punctuate Eric's speech at this point in the play may represent, through the fracturing of his grammar, the way in which the character's mental state is fractured by the revelation of his mother's responsibility for the death of his child. The depth of his feelings for his child convey that despite his initial savagery, Eric is capable of compassion. He is represented as having strong paternal feelings.

The repetition of words like 'child', 'killed' and 'damn', as well as the pronouns, complement this sense of Eric's struggle to control his rationality. The repeated words also focus the audience's attention on the profound nature of Mrs Birling's guilt. Her wrongs are repeated. She has effectively killed a child – her own grandchild – and will be damned to Hell as a result.

The use of the possessive determiners 'my' and 'your' focus attention on the personal nature of this crime. By rejecting social responsibility, Mrs Birling has created a personal tragedy.

The use of the adjective 'own' within the context of 'your own grandchild' is tautologous*. Its only purpose is to emphasise the nature of the close family relationship between Mrs Birling and the child, and to create a sense of guilt in Mrs Birling. As a representative of the older generation and the upper classes, Mrs Birling's refusal to accept her guilt condemns both her and those she represents.

Key Characters

Eric Birling
Sybil Birling

Key Themes

Age
Judgement
Responsibility

Quotation 20 | Act 3

Inspector Goole:

"...as if she were an animal, a thing, not a person."

Analysis

As part of his summation, the Inspector notes Eric's responsibility in the death of Eva Smith. The Inspector appears to adopt a didactic tone at this point. He draws the audience's attention to the sins that the Birlings have committed. Eric may be regarded as symbolising the sin of lust and the Inspector's words emphasise the selfish and degrading nature of this sin. Priestley is not only exploiting the form of the morality play but also appears to be engaging in a more political type of social criticism. Eric's actions could symbolise the rape of the working classes by the capitalist system that the Birlings personify. His behaviour is the opposite of Sheila's statement in Act One that 'these girls aren't cheap labour – they're people.' While Sheila seeks to remind her family of the humanity of the working classes, the behaviour of the Birlings generally strips them of this humanity.

Priestley drives home the appalling nature of Eric's actions by presenting Eva as dehumanised by Eric. The simile has a tripartite structure that is essentially composed of synonyms*. By repeating the same idea in a variety of forms, Priestley makes the terrible treatment of Eva Smith seem inescapable.

Priestley presents Eric as someone who has learned from his mistakes, despite their awful nature. Eric symbolises the younger generation and, along with his sister, he represents, through the acceptance of his responsibility, a hope for the future.

Key Characters

Eva Smith
Inspector Goole

Key Themes

Age
Responsibility
Social Class

Quotation 21 | Act 3

Inspector Goole:

"You made her pay a heavy price for that. And now she'll make you pay a heavier price still."

Analysis

The Inspector summarises Mr Birling's guilt, contextualising his treatment of Eva Smith by reminding him that he refused to pay her a decent wage. Priestley gives a clear sense of the connection between Mr Birling and Eva Smith. This is a specific example of the connection referred to in the Inspector's claim that 'We are responsible for each other.' The connection is reinforced by the use of syntactic parallelism. The grammatical balance reinforces the sense that Mr Birling and Eva Smith are responsible for each other's positions. Birling's punishment is based on his treatment of Eva Smith.

The repetition of 'pay' and 'price' is an ironic use of the semantic field of business. The Inspector criticises Birling in the terms that he understands. This criticism echoes the criticism of Mr Birling by Eric in Act One, when he asks his father 'Why shouldn't they try for higher wages? We try for the highest possible prices.' Now, the same language has transformed from the literal denotation of money and become a metaphorical price. For Eva Smith it is the price of 'death' and for Mr Birling it is the price of 'guilt' or 'damnation'. In this sense, the 'price' is a euphemism*. It is perhaps more powerful in that it refers to the terrible death of Eva Smith that the Inspector has described through dysphemism* elsewhere in the play.

The adjective 'heavy', modifying 'price', gives a sense of a high price. It appears to be an understatement to suggest that Eva Smith's death is merely a 'high price'. However, the repetition of the adjective in its comparative form: 'heavier' suggests that Birling's 'price' will be higher still. A fate worse than death may justify the interpretation of Birling facing damnation as a result of his selfish actions. Within the context of a morality play, Birling symbolises the sin of greed. The Inspector claims that he will pay for this sin.

The contrast between the past and future tense in 'made' and 'make' may complement the idea of paying for actions in the future, a link to Priestley's interest in time and learning from the mistakes of the past. This can be seen in his fascination with the philosophies of Ouspensky* and Dunne*.

Key Characters
Arthur Birling
Inspector Goole

Key Themes
Judgement
Responsibility

Quotation 22 | Act 3

Inspector Goole:

"One Eva Smith has gone – but there are millions and millions and millions of Eva Smiths and John Smiths... with their lives, their hopes and fears, their suffering, and chance of happiness, all intertwined with our lives."

Analysis

The Inspector explicitly refers to the character of Eva Smith as an example of metonymy*. The name 'Eva Smith' represents the idea of a working-class woman. She is *one* Eva Smith because Eva Smiths are representations of working-class women generally. 'Smith' is the most common surname in Britain, a choice that Priestley may have made for the character of Eva in order to more clearly represent her as an 'everyman'. This idea is made even clearer by introducing the notion of 'John Smiths' to metonymically refer to the working classes as a whole.

The death of Eva Smith is euphemistically referred to as 'gone' and the significance of this individual death is lessened by the way in which the Inspector identifies her as one among the many.

The hyperbole of 'millions' of Eva Smiths is complemented by the repetition of the word and the use of polysyndeton* to convey a sense of endlessness. Whether Eva Smith existed as an individual is irrelevant. She is a symbol for the masses, and it is caring for all members of society that the Inspector and Priestley seem to support.

The long list of features of the working class may represent the responsibilities of all members of society to protect these features. The connection between these features and, indeed, all people, is supported by the anaphora* of 'their', a plural pronoun that captures the sense of collectivism and joins clauses together in the same way that Priestley suggests that members of society should be joined. The Inspector does not even distinguish himself from the Birlings. The working classes are 'intertwined' with *our* lives.

Key Characters
Eva Smith
Inspector Goole

Key Themes
Responsibility
Social Class

Quotation 23 | Act 3

Inspector Goole:

"We don't live alone. We are members of one body. We are responsible for each other."

Analysis

The sermonic* style of the Inspector's speech is reinforced by its content at this point in the play. The Inspector's words are very similar to those in the Bible of St. Paul in 1 Corinthians 12: 'For just as the body is one and has many members, and all the members of the body, though many, are one body, so it is with Christ.' Priestley is linking Christian beliefs with his socialist principles and the Inspector, as his mouthpiece, expresses this. Priestley's aim could have been to promote the values of the Labour party. By supporting collective responsibility and the dangers of rejecting it, he defends these ideas. The word 'members' links semantically to the language of politics as well as being a Biblical allusion, just as the word 'body' could metaphorically refer to humanity and an organisation such as the church. Using the image of a body allows Priestley to convey the idea that a failure for the parts to work together compromises the whole body, in the same way that a failure of individuals to work together compromises the whole of society. Priestley may even be referring to what happens when whole groups of people do not work together. The effects are the kinds of wars that Priestley and his audience would have been very aware of.

The need for collective responsibility is presented through a number of Priestley's stylistic choices. The repetition of plural pronouns highlights the social nature of existence while the use of anaphora within the tripartite structure creates a sense of similarity across each of the sentences. Socialism and the principles of the Labour party are based on these ideas of social similarity, or equality.

The Inspector's certainty and power is conveyed through the short sentences and elision. His words and sentence structures are direct and concise, making his message even more forceful.

Key Characters
Inspector Goole

Key Themes
Responsibility
Social Class

Quotation 24	Act 3

Inspector Goole:

"...if men will not learn that lesson, then they will be taught it in fire and blood and anguish..."

Analysis

The final speech of the Inspector, like his dialogue throughout, is hard-hitting and direct. He is no longer only condemning the Birlings, but he widens his criticism to 'men' generally. His use of the third person plural pronoun 'they' conveys that this is a message for the audience and wider humanity. In the National Theatre production, the director chose to position the Inspector to directly address the audience in his closing speech, reinforcing this sense of universal responsibility. Inspector Goole's highly emotive language, coupled with his breaking of the fourth wall*, intensifies guilt and fear in audience members.

As the Inspector states the need for members of society to accept responsibility for their actions, Priestley uses a sermonic register. The Inspector seems to be preaching, using Biblical language that is similar to the descriptions used in the Book of Revelation (8:7) when describing God's apocalyptic judgement of mankind: '...fire mingled with blood...' Priestley is suggesting that if mankind does not learn collective responsibility, then it will suffer punishment on a Biblical scale.

The Inspector's homophonic* name, 'Goole', could support the idea of his final words having spiritual significance. A 'ghoul' is a supernatural being, often used as a synonym for a ghost and usually associated with the recently dead. Goole may be presented as having supernatural powers. He is used by Priestley as a vehicle to warn humanity of the dangers it faces if it does not change its ways. This interpretation could also be supported by the homophonic quality of the root word* 'spector' in the title 'Inspector'; a 'spectre' is also a synonym for a ghost.

Priestley could be using the phrase 'fire and blood and anguish' to create dramatic irony. The play was written in 1945 with its audience having just witnessed the terrible effects of two world wars. However, the play is set in 1912, two years before the start of the First World War. The words 'fire', 'blood' and 'anguish' are all drawn from the semantic field* of war and Priestley's contemporary audience would no doubt recognise the warning that if collective responsibility was not accepted, then war could result. The audience's appreciation that two wars had occurred would act as a powerful lesson regarding the need to show concern for others and a powerful warning that action would have to be taken to maintain peace and avoid further bloodshed. Priestley himself had served in the First World War and therefore recognised the traumatic nature of war. The polysyndetic list of 'fire and blood and anguish' creates a sense of endlessness that could represent the endless horrors of war. Priestley claimed that high ranking officers 'killed' his friends in the war, attributing this to the officers' lack of care for ordinary people. It was this experience that he stated made him feel so passionately about social injustice. Here, Priestley uses the Inspector as a mouthpiece to explore the dangers of failing to take responsibility for others.

Structurally, the quotation's opening conditional clause places the focus on the devastating effects that will occur 'if' his audience does not listen to the Inspector's advice. The parallelism of the verbs 'learn' and 'taught' reinforce the two options that face humanity: learn from past mistakes or be taught through horrific future experiences.

Key Characters

Inspector Goole

Key Themes

Judgement

Responsibility

Quotation 25	Act 3

Sheila Birling:

"So nothing really happened. So there's nothing to be sorry for, nothing to learn. We can all go on behaving just as we did."

Analysis

Sheila's sarcastic response to her father's belief that everything was just as it was before the Inspector's arrival helps to draw attention to the difference between the responses of the younger and older generations. Sheila and Eric have learned something through the inspection, but their parents have not. Priestley appears to be drawing upon the popular theories of time put forward by Dunne and Ouspensky. Ouspensky's belief in constantly recurring events, which some could learn from and reach a higher state of being, is dramatised in the cyclical nature of the play. The play concludes with a phone call that reveals the death of a girl on the way to the infirmary and the imminent arrival of a police inspector, to ask questions, mirroring the opening of the play. Another inspector must 'call' because the older Birlings are continuing to behave 'just as we did', having felt that there was 'nothing to learn'. Sheila and Eric, however, in accepting responsibility, have developed as individuals.

The repetition in Sheila's speech could symbolise the repetition of events in this cyclical narrative. The anaphora of 'So' in the first two sentences is supported by the repetition of 'nothing'. Her sarcastic statements suggest that the younger generation will accept their social responsibilities. They will break the cycle of selfishness, providing some hope for the future. Gerald, however, demonstrates the same inability to learn responsibility as the older Birlings. In another echo of the opening of the play, Gerald offers Sheila the ring once again but Sheila's rejection of this could represent the way in which she will not 'go on behaving just as we did.'

Key Characters

Sheila Birling

Key Themes

Age

Responsibility

Glossary of Key Terms

Ambiguous: Having more than one meaning.

Anagnorisis: In Greek tragedy, the moment of recognition when understanding is reached.

Anaphora: In rhetoric, the repetition of a word or phrase at the beginning of successive clauses.

Article: A word used with a noun to indicate its definiteness. 'The' is the definite article and 'A' is the indefinite article.

Breaking of the fourth wall: Ignoring the imaginary wall that exists between the characters on stage and the audience; this often involves a character addressing the audience directly.

Capitalist: One who supports the political and economic system in which an individual owns the means of production and the distribution of wealth.

Colloquialism: Informal language usually only appropriate for speech.

Conditional clause: A clause that usually begins with 'If' or 'Unless'.

Connotation: An idea or quality inspired by a particular word in addition to the word's meaning.

Conventions: The way that something is usually done or the rules that govern it.

Cyclical: Beginning and ending in the same way.

Denotation: Literal meaning or the thing that a word refers to.

Didactic: Intended to teach, particularly teaching a moral lesson.

Diegetic sound: Sound that originates from the world of the play.

Diminutive: A word, or form of a word, that suggests that something is small.

Dramatic irony: When the audience understands something that the character on stage does not.

Dunne: J. W. Dunne, writer of *An Experiment with Time*.

Dysphemism: A derogatory term used in place of a pleasant or neutral one.

Edwardian: A period in British history, from 1901 to the outbreak of the First World War in 1914 (although Edward only reigned until 1910).

Epistrophe: In rhetoric, the repetition of a word at the end of successive clauses.

Euphemism: A mild or indirect word or expression said instead of one considered to be too harsh or blunt when referring to something unpleasant or embarrassing.

Exclamatory sentence: A statement that conveys excitement or strong emotion, indicated by an exclamation mark.

Homophonic: Two words that sound the same but have a different meaning.

Hyperbolic: Exaggeration.

Idiom: An expression or saying whose meaning is not based on the literal meaning of its constituent words e.g. *kick the bucket* means die.

Imperative: Verb used to give a command.

Interjection: A word or phrase used to show a sudden expression of emotion.

Metonymy: A figure of speech where one thing is replaced with a closely associated word.

Minor sentence: A grammatically incomplete sentence.

Ouspensky: P. D. Ouspensky, philosopher and author of *The Fourth Dimension,* a philosophical consideration of the nature of time.

Parallelism: Grammatical balance, where the structure of a phrase or sentence is mirrored by a similar structure.

Patriarchal: Describing a society controlled by men.

Phonological similarity: Words or parts of words that sound the same.

Politeness codes: The system of expressing good manners.

Polysyndetic: Describing a list in which every clause is separated by a conjunction.

Prejudice: An opinion not supported by experience or reason.

Right-wing: Supporting economic and social conservatism.

Root word: The most basic part of a word, without affixes.

Semantic field: A set of words linked by related meanings.

Sermonic: Having the qualities of a sermon or lesson delivered in a church.

Socialism/Socialist: A political theory in which distribution of wealth should be decided by the community or government.

Synonym: A word that has the same or very similar meaning.

Tautologous: Stating the same thing but using different words to do so.

Unities: Theory based on Aristotle's *Poetics*, that a tragedy should consist of the three singularities of time, place and action.

Well-made play: A neoclassical theatrical genre involving a small number of characters involved in a single action.

Zoomorphic: A metaphor that represents something in the form of an animal.

About the author of this guide

Mark Birch has been a teacher of English for 25 years and the Head of the English Faculty in six schools; he is currently Head of English at Hull Collegiate School. Having achieved his degree at King's College Cambridge, Mark went on to study a PGCE in English at Sheffield University. Mark has been judged as outstanding in every observation of his teaching career and his passion for literary analysis has informed the criticism to be found in this guide. As well as teaching and writing, Mark enjoys producing revision videos that can be found on his YouTube channel.

About the editor of this guide

Hannah Rabey is Head of English at a school in Oxfordshire. Hannah studied Literature and History at the University of East Anglia before studying for her PGCE at the University of Oxford. Hannah is a GCSE examiner and is experienced with teaching all of the texts in the 25 Key Quotations revision guide series.

Printed in Great Britain
by Amazon

57208179R10041